#1
THE
END TIMES
BEGINNING
PHASE

UNDERSTANDING END TIME BIBLE PROPHECY SERIES

DAVID BRENNAN

Understanding End Time Bible Prophecy Series
#1: The End Times Beginning Phase

Website for this book: www.SwordofDavid.com

Published by Teknon Publishing, Metairie, Louisiana

ISBN Number: 978-0-9887614-7-6

Contents

Confession of Faith

I believe in Jesus Christ of Nazareth, placed in the womb of woman by the Spirit of God, crucified on a Roman cross nearly two thousand years ago, died, rose from the dead, and is the resurrection and the eternal life of those placing their trust and faith in Him alone. I believe He is the <u>only</u> way to salvation and place my faith and trust in Him alone for the cleansing of my multitude of sins.

I believe He is the Son of the living God, whom the father sent into the world on a mission of salvation for mankind, overcoming the forces of darkness through His light, guiding believers by the presence of the holy Spirit, and working His holy will not by might nor by power, but by His Spirit.

I believe the Bible is the unerring Word of God, given mankind for salvation and guidance, written through the hand of the prophets guided by the Holy Spirit, the source of truth in a world filled with deception.

I believe all prophetic utterances within the Bible will come to pass in due time.

In Christ,
David Brennan

Key principals employed in this book's approach to Bible prophecy

- God is consistent in His use of terms.
- It is best to allow Scripture to define terms based on their usage.
- It is best to take prophecy Scripture as literally as possible, thereby eliminating the tendency of man to make it say what he wills.
- Scripture alone is the source for truth and not teachers.
- Prophets act as witnesses for the Lord's prophetic truth. As such when several prophets are relaying details to the same event, like all true witnesses one will relay a detail or details that another leaves out.
- Symbolism should be used only as a last resort.

CHAPTER ONE

Starting at the Beginning

Perhaps "starting at the *beginning*" sounds too obvious and doesn't need to be spoken. But in these times with almost as many prophecy theories as there are teachers, starting at the *beginning* phase of what we call the "end times" is probably necessary to stress. Start at the *beginning*. Not in the middle, and not at the end. But at the *beginning* of the end times and use Scripture, and Scripture alone, to understand it. Not teachers. And this approach of starting at the *beginning* is true with almost any learning experience. Think about it. When you go to the library and check out a book why would you skip the first four chapters and begin reading in chapter five? To do so you would miss vital information contained within the first four chapters critical to understanding the book's remaining chapters. Suppose you rented a DVD movie. Would you skip the first 45 minutes and begin watching from that point on? Of course not, because if you did, then much of the movie would not make sense. You start at the *beginning* because it provides a foundation for going forward. And this same concept should be considered true when it comes to the study of Bible prophecy. If you want to obtain an understanding of end time Bible prophecy, then how can you achieve it unless you first have a clear understanding of its *beginning*? The answer: You cannot.

By gaining a clear understanding of the *beginning* of what we call the end times, a person possessing such a foundation will understand where a multitude of Bible prophecy pieces should fit and, just as importantly, where they do not fit. It actually makes understanding the flow of prophetic events somewhat easy by starting at the *beginning* point and then moving forward. And that is the goal of *Understanding End Time Bible Prophecy- #1 The End Times Beginning Phase* … to establish a firm foundation of the *beginning* events of what we call the end times. But this approach is no good if it simply represents the thoughts of a teacher, any teacher, including this one. No, there is only one Teacher whose words count and that is the Lord. And to that point consider that 1 John 2:27 tells us:

But the anointing which you have received from Him abides in you, and you do not need that anyone teach you; but as the same anointing teaches you concerning all things, and is true, and is not a lie, and just as it has taught you, you will abide in Him.

In other words, we should not rely on teachers, but on our Lord and that means looking to His Spirit to guide us through Scripture. So to establish the *beginning* events this book has gathered a multitude of Scripture which relate to the *beginning* phase of what we call the end times. And it does not consider the opinions of teachers.

By gathering together Scriptures that refer to the *beginning* moments of the end times, a picture begins to form that is completely supportable in any Bible prophecy discussion. This is because we are to be guided by Scripture and not teachers. We are told that *all Scripture is good for reproof and correction.* We are not told that a multitude of teachers are good for reproof and correction. So by strictly embracing Scripture, and not teachers, *you will know the truth and it will set you free.* And this is the method employed in the entire *Understanding End Time*

Bible Prophecy series. However, since in our current day many famous and likable TV and radio teachers have been exalted, this approach will be a challenge for some.

There are other methods employed in the *Understanding End Time Bible Prophecy* series that you need to know about. One of them is to allow Scripture to interpret Scripture. Another method employed is to take Scripture very, very, literally but within reason. When, for example, we are specifically told the events described in Matthew 24:4-6 are not a part of *the end*, we will not blend those verses with the events listed in verses 7 & 8 of which we are told is *the beginning*. And, again, when we look at the meaning of prophetic "birth pangs," we will not accept the common definition of it, but will allow Scriptural usage to define it. In other words, we will let the Scriptures tell us what it means and we will simply accept it even though most teachers use a different definition. And one of the reasons why there is an issue with certain prophecy teachings today is because many teachers tend to simply follow what other teachers say about certain Bible prophecy topics, and don't do their homework to confirm it. You will have to decide if you will follow the Scriptural usage, or the consensus of teachers, because in some cases you cannot follow both. The case of what prophetic birth pangs represent is one such test you will face.

It is important to understand that exalting teachers is dangerous for those seeking truth. A perfect example of this took place 2000 years ago when Jesus came to earth. Although the Savior was fulfilling one prophetic Scripture after another, the leading teachers in that day did not recognize Him for who He was. And the reason for this is that they apparently were in a religious echo chamber to busy hearing what the other was saying instead of strictly focusing on Scripture. Had they focused on Scripture alone, and not each other, they would likely have gotten past their pride and recognized that Jesus was their long awaited messiah. And here are a couple of verses related to this approach.

> *2 Peter 1: 20 …knowing this first, that no prophecy of Scripture is of any private interpretation, [21] for prophecy never came by the will of man, but holy men of God spoke as they were moved by the Holy Spirit.*

This Scripture was given to us so that we would reject private and personal interpretations provided by Bible prophecy teachers. One example of how severe private interpreting of prophecy Scripture has become, comes from a well-known Bible prophecy radio show. This show claims that the world has already experienced the first five trumpet judgments in the Book of Revelation. It claims that the first trumpet was fulfilled by "bombs in World War I. Consider the Scripture in question:

> *⁷ The first angel sounded his trumpet,*
> *and there came hail and fire mixed with*
> *blood, and it was hurled down on the*
> *earth. A third of the earth was burned*
> *up, a third of the trees were burned up,*
> *and all the green grass was burned up.*
> *Revelation 8:7*

You heard me correctly. The claim by this radio show is that the *hail and fire mixed with blood* was actually bombs dropped in World War I. This is a perfect example of the kind of *private interpretation* that should be avoided. All Scripture is given to us for *reproof* and *correction* as the following verses tell us.

> *2 Timothy 3:16 All Scripture is given by*
> *inspiration of God, and is profitable for*

doctrine, for reproof, for correction, for instruction in righteousness, [17] that the man of God may be complete, thoroughly equipped for every good work.

So how can any Scripture so distorted as to make *hail and fire mixed with blood* mean bombs be used for any kind of *reproof* and *correction,* if the reader can simply make it mean whatever they want? The answer is that if it can be twisted to such an extent, then it cannot be used for *reproof* and *correction.* Yet, the show doing this has a multitude of followers and donors.

So in our quest to establish the *beginning* events of what we call the end times, we will start by gathering various Scriptures which specifically speak to that *beginning.* And the first set of Scriptures we will look at will be the *beginning* of Jesus' Olivet Discourse which takes the reader from the *beginning* of what we call the end times, all the way to the end. In fact, as will be demonstrated, His Words identify certain events that will happen just before the end times begin. And this is very useful in identifying the point in the Discourse where the end times actually start. What this book will do is to take one Scripture after another that speak to the *beginning* and show

how closely they relate to each other. Thereafter, we will look at the events they describe. As you will notice Scriptural words or phrases in this series are *italicized.*

I encourage you that while reading this book to pray to our Lord Jesus Christ for wisdom, discernment, knowledge, truth, understanding, and revelation. I have prayerfully determined that what I have written here is in line with the Lord's truth. But you have a responsibility to do the same and see if our Lord places it within your heart to accept it. As followers of the Lord we are to seek truth and not the will of any man (teacher). Although I have made every effort to bring together Scripture in a way I believe represents truth, as a man I can be mistaken. It is your responsibility to use discernment and common sense relative to what is written in this book as well as the entire *Understanding End Time Bible Prophecy* series.

David Brennan

Notice to the Reader

Bible prophecy has so many moving parts (Scriptures) which interact with each other, interconnecting and relaying details to the same events, that it can become very confusing at times. What adds to this confusion is the fact that most teachers do not take prophecy Scripture literally which allows them to impart their "interpretation" to it. And this produces a multitude of different interpretations on the same points. That's confusing.

But what you are about to read takes a VERY literal approach to prophecy Scriptures. It also takes a VERY detailed and practical approach to them. And this approach removes any ability to make the Scriptures conform to the will of man allowing the holy Words to speak for themselves.

But the main purpose of this "notice" is to plainly explain the thrust of what you will be reading next. And this is being done in order to make following along with all the interconnecting Scriptures presented a little easier. So take notice that the purpose of the next several chapters is to show the following basic Bible prophecy truth:

- That what we call the end times is, technically speaking, *the day of the Lord* which is the time of God's wrath. That is to say that from the *beginning* moment, until the last moment of what we call the end times, it is *the day of the Lord*. And that within *the day of the Lord* (end times) there is a clear *beginning* phase to it referred to as birth pangs in the prophecy Scriptures.

This understanding will provide you a foundation to understand all end time events. Once you have an appreciation of the interconnecting nature of Matthew 24:7-8, Revelation 6, and 1 Thessalonians 5:1-3, which is covered in the next three chapters, it will be clear that *the day of the Lord* is what we call the end times from start to finish and not some prophetic time frame deep into the 7 year tribulation. And that the 7 year tribulation unfolds within the broader prophetic time frame of *the day of the Lord*. This understanding is critical.

With that understanding you will not only see clearly the events that take place when *the day of the Lord* (end times) begins, but as is shown in book #2 you will know the real signs of its approach.

So remember when you are reading the next several chapters the point being made is that Matthew 24:7-8, Revelation 6, and 1 Thessalonians 5:1-3 are all talking about the same *beginning* of *the day of the Lord* and this is referred to with a birth pangs reference. What is also being shown is the interconnected nature of those Scriptures. Thereafter additional Scriptures will be presented in support of this. But it is the interlocking nature of those 3 Scriptures which remove any doubt that the *beginning* of want we call the end times is the *beginning* of *the day of the Lord* and is referred to with a birth pangs phrase.

CHAPTER TWO

The Beginning Moment of the End Times

Chapter Hint: This chapter begins the process of establishing the *beginning* of the end times by focusing on Matthew 24:7. It identifies that Matthew 24:7, and not the verses before it, are the literal *beginning* of what we call the end times and explains why.

There are only two places in the entire Bible that take the reader through end time prophecy from start to finish. They are the Book of Revelation and the Olivet Discourse found in Matthew 24, Mark 13, and Luke 21. Although there are a multitude of Scriptures found elsewhere that speak to end times prophecy, they each only address a part of it. But the Book of Revelation dedicates twenty-two chapters to the entirety of what we call the end times from its start until its finish.

And the Olivet Discourse also takes the reader from the beginning of the end times, all the way to the end but in only a single chapter. So whereas the Olivet Discourse is a brief summation of events, the Book of Revelation is a detailed description.

<u>Two Places in the Bible covering the end times from start to finish:</u>

1: The Olivet Discourse		2: Book of Revelation
MT 24, LK 21, MK 13	What Chapters	All 22 Chapters
Single Chapter	Obvious Differences	Entire Book
Less detail	Another Difference	Great Detail
Identifies beginning events	Commonality	Identifies beginning events

The Olivet Discourse

Of all the prophetic words spoken by Jesus during His ministry, it is the Olivet Discourse which provides the most detailed and sweeping rendition of the grand events popularly referred to as the end times. His talk begins after being asked by His disciples a very simple question. Their question comes just after Jesus startles them by describing how the massive Jewish

Temple located in Jerusalem, the center of Jewish life in that day, would be destroyed to the point that not one stone would be left upon another. Naturally, after hearing of the impending fate of their precious temple, they not only ask Him when it will happen, but more significantly for current times, *what shall be the sign of thy coming, and of the end of the age?* It is His response to those last two questions that Jesus uses to begin providing a detailed explanation of end time events in what is referred to as the Olivet Discourse.

The approach He takes in answering such an important question is the one any thinking person would employ. He starts by describing the signs that will come just before what He describes as *the beginning.* Then, after describing those signs, He immediately details the actual *beginning* events. By taking this approach it allows Him to very specifically answer their question because He is able to clearly identify the precise events that represent when it all begins. He completely fulfills their request in the spirit of *Ask, and it shall be given you; seek, and ye shall find; knock, and it shall be opened unto you.* They asked a specific question and then received a specific answer. Now for an Olivet Discourse warning.

Some try to say that the Olivet Discourse is directed solely to the Jews. But that cannot be the case. The reason why relates to the last question Jesus is asked … *what shall be the sign … of the end of the age.* We know from Matthew 13 that *the end of the age* represents *the end of the* church *age* as in the removal of the church from the earth thus ending the age of the church. Consider this passage from Matthew 13:37-41 which relates to this usage of this phrase.

> *[37] He answered and said to them: "He who sows the good seed is the Son of Man. [38] The field is the world, the good seeds are the sons of the kingdom, but the tares are the sons of the wicked one. [39] The enemy who sowed them is the devil, <u>the harvest is the end of the age</u>, and the reapers are the angels. [40] Therefore as the tares are gathered and burned in the fire, so it will be at <u>the end of this age</u>. [41] The Son of Man will send out His angels, and they will gather out of His kingdom all things that offend, and those who practice lawlessness,…*

As the passage tells us *the end of the age* is when *the Son of Man* (Jesus) sends out *His angels* to gather His *harvest* ... the church. So clearly that last question of the disciples directly relates to the church and not the Jews. Then Jesus references *the end of the age* three times as His discourse unfolds. So do not let anyone tell you the Olivet Discourse was for the Jews only. This point was necessary to briefly cover before moving on because some people will try to tell you the Olivet Discourse is not directed to the church. But it is.

His Olivet Answer

It is advised that you consider Jesus' words with great care and allow the Scriptures to tell you what He is saying by reading them very literally. The most notable confusion surrounding the next three verses is the belief they are speaking about a vague *beginning* of the end times. But when reading them literally it is clear that Jesus presents two distinct events, within two different prophetic time frames, which creates a clear *beginning* of *the end* times which is able to be identified. That concept is a key understanding. (When we address the Olivet Discourse we will reference Matthew and Luke's renditions.) First consider Matthew 24:6.

> *6And ye shall hear of wars and rumours of wars: see that ye be not troubled: for all these things must come to pass, <u>but the end is not yet.</u>*

After reading this verse several points become clear. The events being described are not part of *the end* times since Jesus states, quite matter-of-factly, *the end is not yet.* In line with that statement He says *be not troubled.* Essentially, He is saying that during the time of *wars and rumours of wars* to *be not troubled* because *the end is not yet.* By taking His words literally there is no other conclusion possible but that the end times have not yet started in this verse. So we will classify the events within this verse as existing within the prophetic pre-birth pangs time frame and the reason for calling it this will soon become obvious. But notice that Jesus does not tell us who is involved in these *wars and rumours of wars.* He only tells a group of Israelites you *shall hear of them.* Now consider Matthew 24:7 and 8.

⁷ For nation shall rise against nation, and kingdom against kingdom: and there shall be famines, and pestilences, and earthquakes, in divers places.

⁸ <u>All these are the beginning of sorrows</u>.

Here, too, several points become immediately clear. By taking Jesus' words literally, it is clear the events discussed in verse 7 mark the start of *the end* times. We know this because after describing a series of signs in verse 7, He then in verse 8 advises us: *All these are the beginning of sorrows*. So what we see is that after describing the events in verses 4-6 as *the end is not yet,* and also nothing to be worried about, He distinguishes verse 7 from those verses. It needs to be noted here that the word used for *beginning of sorrows* in verse 7 is "odin," Greek for birth pangs. As we go along you will see several other Scriptures which use a "birth pangs" term to identify the *beginning* of what we call the end times. That is why we see in this verse the *beginning* moment of *the end* times described by Jesus as birth pangs.

CRITICAL CONCLUSION: THE *WARS AND RUMOURS OF WARS* IN VERSE 6 ARE A

SEPARATE EVENT AND IN A PROPHETIC TIME FRAME PRIOR TO THE NATIONS AND KINGDOMS RISING TO WAR IN VERSE 7.

CRITICAL CONCLUSION: VERSE 7 IS THE LITERAL BEGINNING OF THE END TIMES.

CRITICAL CONCLUSION: JESUS LABELS THE BEGINNING OF THE END TIMES AS <u>BIRTH PANGS.</u>

It is important to note that after describing the events which constitute the *beginning* of *the end* times, Jesus refers to them as "birth pangs." Make a mental note of that. Jesus also makes it clear that this event involves the nations going to war against one another by saying *nation shall <u>rise</u> against nation, and kingdom against kingdom.* We also know this is the actual *beginning* moment of *the end* times since the nations will have to *rise* and, therefore, cannot already at war with one another before verse 7 begins. In other words, something happens which causes them to *rise,* inferring a suddenness to it all. The Greek word used here for *rise* is "egerio" meaning "to arouse, or cause to rise." The nations are suddenly roused to war.

CRITICAL CONCLUSION: BASED ON A LITERAL READING OF JESUS' WORDS, VERSE 7 STARTS THE END TIMES WHICH LAUNCHES WITH A GREAT WAR WHEREIN NATIONS ACROSS THE EARTH *RISE* AGAINST ONE ANOTHER.

Since the nations must literally *rise* when verse 7 and *the end* times begin, then they must have been relatively peaceful going into the start of that verse. Remember, it is nations and kingdoms Jesus literally tells us to consider here. We are not concerned with internal rebellions, revolutions, violent movements, or civil wars. Jesus tells us nations and kingdoms. Put another way, Jesus is describing government entities going to war against one another. And since He makes it clear that the *wars and rumours of wars* in verse 6 are not part of the *beginning* of *the end* times, those wars must be separate and different from the wars described as *nation shall rise against nation*. To blend them together defies Jesus' literal effort to separate them.

The Characteristics of the *Beginning*

So it would appear we can say with confidence that the events mentioned in Matthew 24:7-8 are *the beginning* of what we call *the end* times. We say this by simply believing that Jesus spoke it the way He meant to, and then believing the details of His words. And those events include the following characteristics:

1. Suddenness because the nations must *rise* to war meaning they were not in a state of warfare prior to this moment.
2. It is the *beginning* of what we call the end times.
3. Great destruction because there are wars between nations, earthquakes, pestilence, and famine.
4. And all of this is being described as birth pangs.

Here is a more concise description of those characteristics:

1. Suddenness
2. Beginning
3. Destruction
4. Birth Pangs

David Brennan

Now let's turn to another Scripture which also appears to be describing *the beginning* of the *end times*... Revelation 6.

CHAPTER THREE

Revelation 6: The Beginning of God's Wrath

Chapter Hint: This chapter will show that when the events within Revelation 6 are compared to those of the Olivet Discourse, both describe the same *beginning* events. The case is also presented here that the *beginning* of what we call the end times is, in fact, the *beginning of the day of the Lord...* the time of God's *wrath*. It will also begin the process of establishing that this *beginning of the day of the Lord* is called birth pangs.

The Book of Revelation is noted for its description of terrifying events that will unfold one day. With movies made about it the name itself evokes fear in the hearts of people. But within that book it is not until chapter 6 when the horrific events, typically associated with Revelation, start unfolding in all their colorful descriptions of the four horsemen of the apocalypse bringing destruction. Prior to Revelation chapter 6 there are no descriptions of the type of events that are usually associated with the book. In other words, it is not until chapter 6 when we begin seeing a description of the events relating to the *beginning* of what we call *the end* times. And this means that we should find what is described within that chapter as having similarities to the description of events we just read about in the Olivet Discourse. In making the comparison we will look at both Matthew and Luke's accounts of the Discourse. It is simple common sense that if both prophetic accounts are relaying events concerning a common time frame, *the beginning*, then there should be common descriptions between them. However, keep in mind that we will be comparing events described within the single verse of Matthew 24:7, with the events described in a complete chapter... Revelation 6. This means that Revelation 6 should be expected to offer significantly more detail than Matthew 24:7. So we will look at the broad description of events provided within that single verse of Matthew 24:7, and see if Revelation 6 covers them.

Here is their comparison.

A Great-War

In Matthew 24:7 the first event described is that of warfare. We are told *nation shall rise against nation, and kingdom against kingdom.* Because both nations and kingdoms are described as going to war, it would appear this conflict will be a big one covering all possible government entities. Also, the description of kingdoms and nations are in the plural sense indicating some number of nation states are involved in the conflict.

Now consider what is described in the *second seal* of Revelation 6:

Second Seal: Conflict on Earth

[3] When He opened the second seal, I heard the second living creature saying, "Come and see." [4] Another horse, fiery red, went out. And it was granted to the one who sat on it to take peace from the earth, and that people should kill one another; and there was given to him a great sword.

We are told in the *second seal* that the red horse depicts the removal of *peace from the earth*. And the *sword* granted to the red horse to bring warfare to the earth is a *great* one. This judgment in the *second seal* certainly appears to match Jesus' warning that *nation shall rise against nation, and kingdom against kingdom*.

> (Note that the first seal in Revelation 6, the *white horse*, is a detail not included in the Olivet Discourse. So it is not able to be compared here. But as will be seen later, this appears to be the antichrist conquering as he rises to power.)

Famine

Now consider the *famine* noted in Matthew 24:7. For *famine* to be mentioned by Jesus in His Olivet Discourse, it must be notable and not the average *famine* that has afflicted mankind throughout the ages. Otherwise, how could it be distinguished from the multitude of *famine* events across human history? When we look at Revelation 6 we find that although hunger is specifically indicated in the *fourth seal*, the *third seal* may also relate to it but from an economic standpoint of affordability indicating a scarcity of food.

Third Seal: Scarcity on Earth

> [5] *When He opened the third seal, I heard the third living creature say, "Come and see." So I looked, and behold, a black horse, and he who sat on it had a pair of scales in his hand.* [6] *And I heard a voice in the midst of the four living creatures saying, "A quart of wheat for a denarius, and three quarts of barley for a denarius; and do not harm the oil and the wine."*

It is indicated in the *third seal* that a day's wages, *a denarius*, will be the cost for *A quart of wheat, and three quarts of barley.* This is an extremely expensive cost for these products indicating that great inflation has arrived probably due to the scarcity of these food items. And wheat, being a basic food staple, is included here. However, although hunger is alluded to in this passage, it is within the *fourth seal* where hunger is specifically identified.

Hunger & Pestilence

In addition to *hunger* being identified in the *fourth seal*, we also see *pestilence*, which Jesus indicated in Matthew 24:7. Such *pestilence* would be the natural outgrowth from the death and destruction of warfare identified in the *second seal*. In fact, it is also likely that the notable hunger would also result from a great-war. Typically, in the aftermath of a great-war, the plagues of hunger and *pestilence* follow because of the death and destruction wars bring. Consider what happens when the *fourth seal* is opened.

Fourth Seal: Widespread Death on Earth

> [7] *When He opened the fourth seal, I heard the voice of the fourth living creature saying, "Come and see."* [8] *So I looked, and behold, a pale horse. And the name of him who sat on it was Death, and Hades followed with him. And power was given to them over a fourth of the earth, to kill with sword, with hunger, with death, and by the beasts of the earth.*

This particular judgment includes a multitude of devastating events that come upon the earth. For one thing we are told that over a *fourth of the earth* there is warfare, as well as *hunger*, (*famine*) and *the beasts of the earth*. And this term, *the beasts of the earth*, is likely referring to pestilence and not lions, tigers, and bears attacking people in mass. One question raised by this judgment is if the warfare is additional to the warfare and hunger mentioned in the second and third seals or a reiteration of them. But it is likely that this is additional warfare, *hunger*, and *pestilence* since it is being described in a separate and additional judgment.

Earthquake

In Luke's rendition of the Olivet Discourse he describes the *earthquakes in divers places* as *great* ones. Revelation 6 also notes *a great earthquake*:

> *¹² I looked when He opened the sixth seal, and behold, there was a <u>great earthquake</u>; and the sun became black as sackcloth of hair, and the moon became like blood. ¹³ And the stars of heaven fell to the earth,*

as a fig tree drops its late figs when it is shaken by a mighty wind.

Cosmic Disturbances

It is not uncommon for one prophet to relay details pertaining to the same event that another prophet leaves out. This is a notable characteristic common among true witnesses to any event. And in the case of the Olivet Discourse we have such an instance to include here. In Matthew's account we hear nothing about any kind of cosmic event in the *beginning* of his rendition of the Olivet Discourse. However, in Luke's account we do. Consider the following Scripture from Luke 21 which covers the same ground as Matthew 24:7 but adds a particular detail relating to the cosmos.

¹⁰ Then said he unto them, Nation shall rise against nation, and kingdom against kingdom:

¹¹ And great earthquakes shall be in divers places, and famines, and pestilences; <u>and fearful sights and great signs shall there be from heaven.</u> Luke 21:10-11

Luke's account tells us of some kind of fearful sights relating to the heavens. Exactly what these *fearful sights* are we are not told. Now consider Revelation 6:12-14

> ¹² *And I beheld when he had opened the sixth seal, and, lo, there was a great earthquake; and the sun became black as sackcloth of hair, and the moon became as blood;*
>
> ¹³ <u>*And the stars of heaven fell unto the earth, even as a fig tree casteth her untimely figs, when she is shaken of a mighty wind.*</u>
>
> ¹⁴ <u>*And the heaven departed as a scroll when it is rolled together; and every mountain and island were moved out of their places.*</u>

The reason why these verses may be referencing an actual cosmic disturbance is in the details of its description. When we are told in verse 13 ... *the stars of heaven fell to the earth, as a fig tree drops its late figs when it is shaken by a mighty wind,* there is little doubt that this cannot be the literal *stars* in the galaxy or solar system falling to the earth. So the verse is referencing something happening in the heavens that apparently resembles *stars* falling to the earth like so many ripe figs from a tree *shaken by a mighty wind.*

We are told in verse 14 *the sky receded as a scroll when it is rolled up.* That is an unusual description of the view of the sky. So we have a multitude of objects that look like *stars* falling to the earth and people can clearly see them. And there is also an atmospheric event taking place at the same time wherein a large segment of the sky is methodically disappearing from sight so that it appears like a *scroll* being *rolled up.* Then we are given another clue in the last half of verse 14 when we are told *every mountain and island was moved out of its place.* That indicates a massive earth shaking event taking place either relating to earthquakes or a gravitational impact on the earth. Since the other descriptions are all related to an astronomical event, then it may be a celestial object's gravitational pull on the earth creating some great earthquakes. This is speculation but appears to have a logic behind it. Now consider the reaction of people on the earth as these unusual events in the sky are unfolding. We are told …

*...the kings of the earth, the great men,
the rich men, the commanders, the mighty
men, every slave and every free man, hid
themselves in the caves and in the rocks of
the mountains.*

The reaction of people on the earth to what is happening in the sky above them is to flee to *caves*. This would seem to add credibility to the case that whatever these *stars* are that are falling to the earth, like a ripe *fig tree drops its late figs when it is shaken by a mighty wind*, are endangering people on the ground. In book *#3 Heavenly Signs & Cosmic Disturbances* the case is made that only a very large asteroid or comet passing very close to the earth would be able to fulfill all of these Scriptural descriptions in Revelation 6. And this would certainly match up with Luke telling us about *fearful sights* in the heavens.

Now consider how well the events listed in Revelation 6 compare to the listing of *beginning* events in the Olivet Discourse.

Olivet Discourse	Vs.	Book of Revelation
End Time		End Time
Beginning Events		Beginning Events

	Antichrist Rises
Great-War	Great-War
Famines	Famines
Pestilences	Pestilences
Earthquakes	Great Earthquake
Fearful Heavenly Sights	*Stars* falling to earth

Conclusion

So we can conclude, based on the comparison of the two, that although Revelation chapter 6 has more details within it than Matthew 24:7, both are referring to the same events in the *beginning* of the end times. This is because all of the events within the Olivet Discourse are contained within Revelation 6. Revelation 6 simply supplies more details because it is a full chapter compared to the single verse of Matthew 24:7 or the two verses of Luke 21:10-11. And both are clearly *beginning* events. Now consider the description provided at the end of Revelation 6 which tells us what the events within it prophetically represent.

The Wrath of God

After describing the litany of terrible events in chapter 6 including the four horsemen of the apocalypse, which match Jesus' description of events detailed in the Olivet Discourse, at the end of the chapter the author is ready to describe what those events represent.

Revelation 6:16-17

[16] and said to the mountains and rocks, "Fall on us and hide us from the face of Him who sits on the throne and from the <u>wrath of the Lamb</u>! [17] For <u>the great day of His wrath has come</u>, and who is able to stand?"

We have just been told that the events in Revelation chapter 6 are the *wrath* of God. In fact, it is described as *the great day of His wrath*. And this makes sense because all of the horrific events described and unleashed in Revelation 6, including the four horsemen of the apocalypse, were unleashed by the hand of Jesus in heaven by opening seals on a scroll. Of course, this is the *wrath* of God. How can it be anything other than the *wrath* of God since it is unleashed by the hand of Jesus from heaven? (Some say this cannot be the start of the wrath of God-*the Day of the Lord*, because of the heavenly sign/condition indicated in the chapter. However, the case against them is addressed in Addendum 1 in the back of the book. In fact, this heavenly sign/condition is exactly what should be expected <u>during</u> the time of God's wrath … *the day of the Lord* and not <u>before</u> it. This is covered in detail in book *#3: Heavenly Signs & Cosmic Disturbances*.)

So here are some of the main characteristics of Revelation 6:

1. The destruction described in Revelation 6 is not proceeded by any prior destructive events and, therefore, it is the *beginning* of prophetic end time destruction described in the Book of Revelation.
2. The Book of Revelation does not prepare the reader for the onslaught of destruction that appears in chapter 6, but introduces it with no forewarning. A first time reader of the book would not know that the opening of the seals

are about to unleash hell on earth, so there is a suddenness associated with the destruction.

3. There is great destruction described by what the four horsemen of the apocalypse do to the earth.

4. This event is summed up at the end of the chapter as the *wrath* of God

Here is a more concise description of the characteristics associated with Revelation chapter 6:

1. Suddenness
2. Beginning
3. Destruction
4. Wrath of God

Notice how similar these characteristics are to what we saw in Matthew 24:7-8. Here are those characteristics again.

1. Suddenness
2. Beginning
3. Destruction
4. Birth Pangs

The only obvious differences is that what the Olivet Discourse refers to as birth pangs, Revelation

6 calls the wrath of God. Revelation 6 also is able to supply more details since it covers an entire chapter relaying *beginning* events that Jesus describes in a single verse in Matthew 24:7. However, in spite of how short the *beginning* description of events are in Matthew 24:7-8, we find Revelation 6 checks off each one. And since both Matthew 24:7 and Revelation 6 represent *beginning* events, then we must believe both are relaying events within the same prophetic time frame… the *beginning*.

Wrath and Birth Pangs

Whereas Matthew 24:7-8 describe their *beginning* events as prophetic birth pangs, Revelation 6 describes its *beginning* events as the *wrath* of God. And we know that throughout the Bible the Scriptures describing the *wrath* of God are referred to as *the day of the Lord*. Therefore, we have Revelation 6 describing the same events as Matthew 24:7 but instead of referring to them as birth pangs, they are referred to as the *wrath* of God which we know is *the day of the Lord*. (If you are one who thinks the events in Revelation 6 cannot be *the day of the Lord* because of the heavenly sign mentioned near the end of the chapter, then go read

Addendum 1 in the back of the book to see what is tripping you up.)

Marrying Birth Pangs and Wrath

So let's now look at 1 Thessalonians 5:1-3 which also describes *beginning* events. However, it will add to our understanding by marrying the terms birth pangs with *the day of the Lord* and act as further confirmation that all three Scriptures; Matthew 24:7, Revelation 6, and 1 Thessalonians 5:1-3, are relaying events in the same prophetic time frame… the *beginning*.

CHAPTER FOUR

Birth Pangs & The Day of the Lord

Chapter Hint: This chapter confirms that the *beginning* of the end times is the *beginning* of the wrath of God, *the day of the Lord,* and is referred to as birth pangs and is a separate prophetic time frame from all other end time events.

U nderstanding prophetic time frames is critically important in avoiding the confusion that plagues so many students of Bible prophecy. In fact, to establish a strong Bible prophecy foundation, it is critical to understand that there is a *beginning* time frame to what we call the end times. We just saw that Matthew 24:7 clearly identifies the actual *beginning* time frame, and that Revelation 6 is in broad agreement with those same *beginning* events described in Matthew 24:7. But the critical take away from that discovery is the label attached to their respective events. In Matthew 24 and Luke 21 we see these *beginning* events described as birth pangs. And in Revelation 6 we see the events described as the *wrath* of God which we know is, by definition, *the day of the Lord*. (See addendum 2 in the back of the book for a litany of *day of the Lord* Scriptures to confirm this definition) Now we find within 1 Thessalonians 5:1-3 that birth pangs is the term used to describe the *beginning* of *the day of the Lord*.

1 Thessalonians 5:1-3

For you yourselves know perfectly that <u>the day of the Lord</u> so cometh as a thief in the night. ³ For when they shall say, Peace and safety; then sudden destruction cometh upon them, <u>as travail upon a woman with child</u>; and they shall not escape.

Because the term *the day of the Lord* is used we know that this Scripture is addressing the time of God's wrath and we also found it was His wrath in Revelation 6. Additionally, because the phrase *as travail upon a woman with child* was used we can understand that it also relates to the *beginning* events described in Matthew 24:7 as birth pangs. And just like Jesus in Matthew 24:8 the Greek word "odin" is used here to signify those birth pangs. So both Jesus in Matthew 24:7-8, and Paul in 1 Thessalonians 5:1-3, describe their events as prophetic birth pangs. And notice when Paul uses the term birth pangs he associates it with *sudden destruction*.

Since we see both Jesus and Paul using the same birth pangs term to describe their respective events, it begs the following question: Would Jesus use a birth pangs term to describe the *beginning of sorrows* and then the Holy Spirit guide Paul to use the birth pangs term to describe events in some time frame other than the *beginning*? Adding to the case that the Holy Spirit is consistent in the use of this term is the fact that when it is used in Matthew and Luke we are told the nations will *rise* to go to war. As mentioned earlier this means they could not already be in a general state of warfare prior to that moment because they must *rise* to war when the verse begins. That is consistent with what we are being told in 1 Thessalonians 5 where destruction comes suddenly with the words, *then sudden destruction cometh upon them,* which logically infers the nations receiving this *sudden destruction* were not already in a state of warfare prior to its *beginning*. Jesus and Paul both appear to be talking about the same event wherein the nations must *rise* to war in Matthew 24 and Luke 21, which is the *sudden destruction* described in 1 Thessalonians 5:1-3. War is destruction and the need to *rise* represents a sudden move. *Webster's Dictionary* defines *rise* in this context as "to take up arms." So both Jesus in Matthew 24:7, and Paul in 1 Thessalonians 5:1-3, infer suddenness when using the term birth pangs and they both appear to be describing the same *beginning* event.

Adding to the case that the Holy Spirit is consistent in using the birth pangs term to denote the *beginning* of the end times, we are told the *sudden destruction* in 1 Thessalonians 5 *cometh as a thief in the night*, which amplifies its suddenness. But consider this. If this is not the opening event of the end times, then how could it come with such surprise? Remember, during the end times along with great physical destruction of property, a large portion of the world's population is lost. Within such an environment how could this verse unfold with the suddenness of *a thief in the night* if it occurs deep into the end times after so many horrific events have already occurred? It could not. It is only during the *beginning of sorrows* that such surprise is possible. In strategic terms this is called the "element of surprise." Once great cataclysms begin unfolding, the element of surprise is lost forever.

The Same Beginning Characteristics

Both Jesus and Paul painstakingly set out to describe their respective events as the *beginning* of the end times and then label them birth pangs. But Paul does something else as well. He tells us that this *sudden destruction* represents the launch of *the day of the Lord*. And by definition *the day of the Lord* is the time of God's wrath. Remember the events described in Revelation 6, which fit the events described in Olivet Discourse, were also described as the wrath of God? We have strong synergy between the *beginning* events described in Matthew 24:7-8, Revelation 6, and 1 Thessalonians 5:1-3. So here are some of the main characteristics being described in 1 Thessalonians 5:1-3:

1. There is a <u>suddenness</u> associated with these events.
2. This event is a clear *<u>beginning</u> event* since it is describing the start of *the day of the Lord*. (God's wrath)

3. There is <u>destruction</u> since the Scripture tells us there will be *sudden destruction*.
4. It is the *beginning* of <u>God's wrath</u> because it is described as *the day of the Lord* which, by definition, is the time of God's wrath.

Here is a more concise description of the characteristics associated with what we just read 1 Thessalonians 5:1-3

1. Suddenness
2. Beginning
3. Destruction
4. Wrath of God
5. Described as birth pangs

If this description of main characteristics looks familiar it should. It is nearly identical to the main characteristics that we identified in Matthew 24:7-8 and Revelation 6. Remember that both of those Scriptures also described *beginning* events so naturally they should have much in common with 1 Thessalonians 5:1-3. And they do. Whereas Matthew 24:7 refers to its *beginning* events as prophetic birth pangs, Revelation 6 describes it as the wrath of God. That is why we see 1 Thessalonians 5:1-3 using both the terms birth pangs and *the day of the Lord*. (Wrath of God) It is because the context of these Scriptures is establishing that there is a *beginning* phase to *the day of the Lord* (End times) which is referred to as birth pangs. Now consider how the structure of the Book of Revelation speaks to this birth pangs *beginning* phase to *the day of the Lord* as being separate from all remaining events within that book.

The Structure of Revelation

Remember that all horrific events catalogued in the Book of Revelation flow from the *seven seals* loosened by Jesus. Make certain you have that understood. Let me repeat. All judgments that unfold within the Book of Revelation are unleashed from the *seven seals*. Now consider the sequence of the opening of those *seven seals* because it is divided between the first six seals being distinctly separate from the opening of the seventh seal. All of the *beginning* events listed in Revelation chapter 6, which match the birth pangs of *the day of the Lord,* are unleashed from the first six of those *seven seals*. The *seventh seal* is not included. The *seventh seal* does not open until chapter 8 and is completely separate from the first six seals. And from that *seventh seal* come all remaining judgments… the seven trumpet judgments as well as the seven vial judgments. In other words, after the first six seals are loosened in chapter 6, and match the birth pangs of Matthew 24:7, the remaining fifteen judgments are separate from them and do not start until chapter 8. Then from chapter 8 until chapter 16 those remaining fifteen judgments unfold. So the structure of the Book of Revelation speaks to the distinct nature of the birth pangs *beginning* phase of *the day of the Lord* as being separate from the remainder of events in that book. (For an in depth perspective on the flow and structure of the Book of Revelation read book #5.) Now let's briefly take a look at the term birth pangs for a fuller perspective on it. Here is the critical take away from this chapter.

CRITICAL CONCLUSION: PROPHETIC BIRTH PANGS ARE THE *BEGINNING* PHASE OF *THE DAY OF THE LORD* AND SEPARATE FROM ALL REMAINING JUDGMENTS.

CHAPTER FIVE

More on Prophetic Birth Pangs

Chapter Hint: This chapter will continue to establish that prophetic birth pangs are, in fact, the *beginning* phase of *the day of the Lord* (end times). However, it will take another step. It will show that *the day of the Lord* stretches all the way from the *beginning* moment of what we call the end times, until the ending moment. It also continues to establish that prophetic birth pangs do not unfold before the "end times" (*day of the Lord*) begin as some teach, but <u>are</u> its *beginning*. This gives you a basic framework under which all "end time" (*the day of the Lord*) prophecy operates within.

By understanding that the *beginning* of *the day of the Lord* is the *beginning* of what we call the end times, you also gain the added benefit of knowing exactly what geopolitical and astronomical warning signs take place just before it starts. That means you cannot be fooled by those trying to sell you a book or DVD making claims that a prophetic event is about to take place. You will be able to use Scripture to rebuke or confirm the Bible prophecy claims of others. And you will be able to use Scripture for reproof and correction in any prophecy discussion knowing your position is strongly supported by Scripture. Now we will continue looking at more details about prophetic birth pangs.

We have reasoned that any Scriptures speaking to the same prophetic time frame should have many similarities when comparing their respective events. And, in fact, that is exactly what we have found after looking at Matthew 24:7, 1 Thessalonians 5:1-3, and Revelation 6. In Matthew 24:7-8 we saw the following characteristics associated with "birth pangs."

1. Suddenness
2. Beginning
3. Destruction
4. Wrath of God

5. Birth Pangs

In 1 Thessalonians 5:1-3 we saw that *the day of the Lord* will come suddenly, with *destruction*, and is described as prophetic birth pangs. That suddenness was matched in Matthew 24:7 when we were told the nations and kingdoms going to war would have to *rise*. So consider again the following characteristics associated with the birth pangs described in 1 Thessalonians 5:1-3.

1. Suddenness
2. Beginning
3. Destruction
4. Wrath of God
5. Birth Pangs

And since we made the connection between the Olivet Discourse and Revelation 6, we know both have to be referring to the wrath of God which is, by definition, *the day of the Lord*. In so doing we see complete commonality between the Olivet Discourse (Matthew 24 and Luke 21), Revelation 6, and 1 Thessalonians 5:1-3. However, there are more Scriptures that use the birth pangs term. So let's see what characteristics they possesses. One such

Scripture is Isaiah 42. Although it relates to events long ago, it is useful for seeing the common usage of the birth pangs term when the wrath of God came down in the past.

Isaiah 42:1 4

I have long time holden my peace; I have been still, and refrained myself: now will I cry like a <u>travailing woman</u>; I will destroy and devour at once.

[15] I will make waste mountains and hills, and dry up all their herbs; and I will make the rivers islands, and I will dry up the pools.

We are told in these verses that the Lord has held His *peace*, and been *still, and reframed*. And He has been doing this for a *long time*. However, it appears that His patience has run out and He is finally ready to act by bringing His wrath because we are told He will *devour at once*. This sudden *beginning* of His *wrath* is being described as birth pangs. The term used here for birth pangs is the Hebrew verb "yalad" which means: to bear, bring forth, beget, of child birth. It is a birth pangs term. Now consider the characteristics associated with it usage.

1. He has held His peace but then will devour at once. This is suddenness.
2. It is also the *beginning* of His actions against them because He has held His peace but will no more.
3. He destroys which is destruction.
4. It is the Lord's wrath.
5. It is described as birth pangs.

A summation of these characteristics is as follows:

1. Suddenness
2. Beginning
3. Destruction
4. Wrath of God
5. Birth pangs

These are the exact same characteristics associated with prophetic birth pangs we saw in the Olivet Discourse, Revelation 6, and 1 Thessalonians 5:1-3 which all related to God's wrath within end time events. The only difference is that the wrath of God being described in Isaiah 42 does not relate to the end times. But when God's wrath is related to what we call the end times, it is referred to as *the day of the Lord*. So when we look strictly at the Scriptural usage of the term birth pangs we get a clear definition. And this definition is in conflict with many current day teachings. This is why you were forewarned in the beginning of this book that there would come points herein where you would have to choose between what Scripture plainly says, and what is taught by certain teachers. This is one of those times. Therefore, based strictly on Scriptural usage the correct definition of the term birth pangs, <u>when used in a *day of the Lord* context</u>, is as follows:

THE SUDDEN BEGINNING OF GOD'S WRATH

In more common language:

THE SUDDEN BEGINNING OF THE END TIMES

It is equally clear that prophetic birth pangs are not events that happen before the end times (*day of the Lord*) leading up to its *beginning* as so many teach. But they are, in fact, the *beginning* itself. This distinction is critical to properly understanding what events occur in the actual *beginning* of the end times, and what events happen just before it begins acting as warning signs.

Keep in mind that this definition of birth pangs was derived not from teachers, but directly from Scriptural usage. And it informs us that the *beginning* of what we call the end times is, actually, the *beginning* of *the day of the Lord...* the time of God's wrath. So when we see a birth pangs term used within a Scripture, associated with end time events, we can understand it too must also be referring to the *sudden beginning* of God's *wrath*. In other words, such Scriptures will add to our understanding of the *beginning* of *the day of the Lord* (end times).

Derived from Scriptural Usage

At this point you should be able to see clearly why it was so important to establish the correct definition of the term prophetic birth pangs. Without this understanding it is not possible to comprehend end time Bible prophecy. In order to understand end time Bible prophecy you have to establish a foundation of the *beginning* events in order to move forward. So having shown that the *beginning* of what we call the end times is, in reality, the start of *the day of the Lord,* it is important to gain the proper perspective on *the day of the Lord.* So here is a question relating to it:

Over what portion of the end times does *the day of the Lord* span?

To that question we already have part of the answer. From what we have just studied, we know that *the day of the Lord* launches the *beginning* of what we call the end times. We know this from the Olivet Discourse (Matthew 24 and Luke 21), 1 Thessalonians 5:1-3, and Revelation 6. Each Scripture very specifically describes *beginning* events and have great synergy between them. By allowing the Scriptures to speak we simply accept what they are saying without complicating it. However, the next four verses from the prophet Zechariah establish how broad and all-encompassing *the day of the Lord* actually is. Whereas we just saw the Olivet Discourse, 1 Thessalonians 5:1-3, and Revelation 6 relay information on events that take place at the *beginning* of *the day of the Lord,* we will next see that Zechariah14 provides a snapshot of an event that will happen at the end of *the day of the Lord* with his focus on the return of Jesus. (This is being shown to make the point that *the day of the Lord* encompasses all of what we call the end times from start to finish.) The prophet is not interested in any other moment relating to *the day of the Lord* except the tail end of it. And, of course, because of this he does not use a birth pangs reference because this is not an event happening in the *beginning.* Consider Zechariah 14:1-4 titled in the New King James version: "The Day of the Lord."

> *¹Behold, <u>the day of the LORD</u> is coming, And your spoil will be divided in your midst.*
>
> *² For I will gather all the nations to battle against Jerusalem; The city shall be taken, The houses rifled, And the women ravished. Half of the city shall go into captivity, But the remnant of the people shall not be cut off from the city.*
>
> *³ Then the LORD will go forth And fight against those nations, As He fights in the day of battle.*
>
> *⁴ <u>And in that day His feet will stand on the Mount of Olives</u>, Which faces Jerusalem on the east. And the Mount of Olives shall be split in two, From east to west, Making a very large valley; Half of the*

mountain shall move toward the north
And half of it toward the south.

I have underlined the key part of these Scriptures which allow us to establish the time frame that Zechariah is writing about. When he tells us, <u>*And in that day His feet will stand on the Mount of Olives,*</u> the prophet is referring to Jesus Christ's return to the earth. It is Jesus who at the end of the seven year tribulation will return to earth and stand on the Mount of Olives. Because this event takes place at the tail end of the seven year tribulation, (end times) we have a time marker here at the very end of what is popularly called the end times. And yet these events are also clearly described as *the day of the Lord.* And, of course, there is no mention of birth pangs here because this event happens at the end of *the day of the Lord* and not in the *beginning.* We know from a multitude of Scripture that *the day of the Lord* launches the *beginning* of what we call the end times, and we now see a Scripture that shows it is still *the day of the Lord* at the end of what is popularly called the end times. But here is a note of caution.

Some people try to say that *the day of the Lord* unfolds only over a portion of the seven-year tribulation. One Scripture that trips them up is Isaiah 34:8 which reads:

> *For it is the day of the Lord's vengeance,*
> <u>*the year of recompense*</u> *for the cause of*
> *Zion.*

However, because we have already established the *beginning* moment of *the day of the Lord* as occurring at the *beginning* of what popularly call the end times, and Zechariah 14 tells us it is still *the day of the Lord* at the tail end of the same, then we know *the day of the Lord* is what we call the end times from start to finish. Notice the Isaiah 34:8 reference to the *year of recompense* has no birth pangs phrase and contextually fits well with the events described in Zechariah 14 that we know take place at the end of the seven year tribulation. And it is notable that *Zion* is another word for *Jerusalem* which adds to the case that this statement is referring to the same events as Zechariah 14 which also references actions against *Jerusalem*. In fact, the word for *recompense* in the verse is the Hebrew masculine noun "shilluwm," which means "retribution" which relays back to the Lord's actions against the nations for what they have done to *Jerusalem*. All Isaiah 34:8 is doing is describing what appears to be the last year of retribution against the nations at the end of the seven year tribulation.

The purpose of pointing this out is to make certain you are not tripped up into thinking *the day of the Lord* spans only one year at the end of the seven year tribulation. So this statement in Isaiah 34 about the *year of recompense* appears to be simply referring to the last year of *the day of the Lord* as the *year of recompense for Zion*... which is another way of saying *Jerusalem* which is the focus of Zechariah 14 as well. Also we see Zechariah 12 talking about the same event as Zechariah 14 but providing additional perspectives. And it too mentions the appearance of Jesus at the end of *that day* ... another way of saying *the day of the Lord* and adds another Scripture establishing it is still *the day of the Lord* when the end of the seven ear tribulation comes.

> *¹ The burden of the word of the LORD against Israel. Thus says the LORD, who stretches out the heavens, lays the foundation of the earth, and forms the spirit of man within him:*
>
> *² "Behold, I will make Jerusalem a cup of drunkenness to all the surrounding*

peoples, when they lay siege against Judah and Jerusalem.

³ And it shall happen in that day that I will make Jerusalem a very heavy stone for all peoples; all who would heave it away will surely be cut in pieces, though all nations of the earth are gathered against it.

⁴ In <u>that day</u>," says the LORD, "I will strike every horse with confusion, and its rider with madness; I will open My eyes on the house of Judah, and will strike every horse of the peoples with blindness.

Mourning for the Pierced One

¹⁰ "And I will pour on the house of David and on the inhabitants of Jerusalem the Spirit of grace and supplication; then they will look on Me whom they pierced. Yes, they will mourn for Him as one mourns for his only son, and grieve for Him as one grieves for a firstborn.

Here too we see references to events that happen at the end of the seven year tribulation and it is still *that day,* another way of referencing *the day of the Lord.* We see a warning against the nations surrounding *Jerusalem* just as we did in Zechariah 14. And we also see the appearance of Jesus. So both Zechariah 14 & 12 are showing that it is still *the day of the Lord* at the end of what we call the end times. Therefore, since we also saw an array of Scriptures making it clear that the *beginning* of what we call the end times is the start of *the day of the Lord,* and now we see Scriptures which tell us it is still *the day of the Lord* during the concluding events, we reach the following critical conclusion:

CRITICAL CONCLUSION: *The day of the Lord* is the end times from its beginning moment, until its last moment.

In other words…

Everything we call the end times including the seven year tribulation is, in reality, *the day of the Lord* … the time of God's wrath.

Now consider more Scriptures that relate to the *beginning* of *the day of the Lord* by using a birth pangs phrase. These Scriptures provide additional perspectives on that prophetic time frame and further confirm what we have just learned.

CHAPTER SIX

More Birth Pangs: Isaiah 13 & Jeremiah 30

Chapter Hint: This chapter looks at more Scriptures which use the birth pangs phrase for additional confirmation of the definition we are using. And also for more conformation that the *beginning* of what we call the end times is the start of *the day of the Lord* reaffirming that *the day of the Lord* covers the entirety of what we call the end times from start to finish.

There is another Scripture in the Book of Isaiah which references the time of prophetic birth pangs. And in this case it is directly associated with *the day of the Lord* so it is completely in line with what we are looking at here. Based on the various Scriptures we have studied, this means the events it is describing should relate to the *beginning*. Here is Isaiah 13:6-8.

> Isaiah 13
>
> [6] *Wail, for <u>the day of the LORD</u> is at hand! It will come as <u>destruction from the Almighty</u>.*
>
> [7] *Therefore all hands will be limp, Every man's heart will melt,*
>
> [8] *And they will be afraid. Pangs and sorrows will take hold of them; They will be <u>in pain as a woman in childbirth</u>; They will be amazed at one another; Their faces will be like flames.*

Isaiah 13:6-8 is discussing *the day of the Lord* and specifically attaches a birth pangs term to it with the phrase *in pain as a woman in childbirth*. It is the same Hebrew verb "yalad" we saw in Isaiah 42. Here are the general characteristics associated with this passage:

1. Destruction

2. Wrath of God
3. Birth Pangs

Although suddenness is not included within this passage, most of the other main characteristics we have looked at are. We see that the first verse in this chapter references Babylon saying, *The burden against Babylon which Isaiah the son of Amoz saw,* but the passages quickly blend into describing *the day of the Lord.* How do we know this is not strictly speaking about ancient Babylon? Because in addition to *the day of the Lord* being specifically mentioned, we also find a clear reference to the heavenly condition that will exist during the unfolding of *the day of the Lord.* This is what we are told a few verses later:

Isaiah 13:9

Behold, the day of the Lord *comes, Cruel, with both wrath and fierce anger, To lay the land desolate; And He will destroy its sinners from it.*

[10] For the stars of heaven and their constellations Will not give their light; The sun will be darkened in its going

> *forth, And the moon will not cause its*
> *light to shine.:*

In book *#3 Heavenly Signs & Cosmic Disturbances* we find that <u>during</u> *the day of the Lord* the sun, moon, and stars are all three impacted. This notable heavenly <u>condition</u> is peculiar to *the day of the Lord* and is not to be confused with the heavenly <u>sign</u> that comes just before *the day of the Lord* begins. (Before *the day of the Lord* only the sun and moon are impacted) Part of the reason why all celestial bodies are impacted during *the day of the Lord* is the condition of the atmosphere during that time. This is covered in detail in book *#3 Heavenly Signs & Cosmic Disturbances*. But the point of mentioning this is that these verses in Isaiah 13 if some of them apply to ancient Babylon must also apply to *the day of the Lord*. (End times) And the whole point of this is to show that, once again, some of the common characteristics relating to the prophetic birth pangs of *the day of the Lord* are present. Now let's look at Jeremiah 30:6-8 which refers to *the day of the Lord* by using the terms *that day*, as well as the term *time of Jacob's trouble*.

⁶ Ask now, and see, Whether a man is ever in labor with child? So why do I see every man with his hands on his loins like <u>a woman in labor,</u> And all faces turned pale?

⁷ Alas! For <u>that day is great,</u> So that none is like it; And it is the <u>time of Jacob's trouble,</u> But he shall be saved out of it.

⁸ 'For it shall come to pass in <u>that day,</u>' Says the L<small>ORD</small> of hosts, 'That I will break his yoke from your neck, and will burst your bonds; Foreigners shall no more enslave them.

Then, a few verses later...

¹¹ For I am with you,' says the L<small>ORD</small>, 'to save you; Though <u>I make a full end of all nations</u> where I have scattered you, Yet I will not make a complete end of you. But I will correct you in justice, And will not let you go altogether unpunished.'

So this is what we get from Jeremiah 30 which tells us these verses apply to the *beginning* of *the day of the Lord* (end times) as well.

1. Destruction
2. Wrath of God
3. Birth pangs

In the next chapter we will begin looking at all of the general and specific events that will happen when *the day of the Lord* (end times) begins. And what you are about to read is based strictly on Scripture. It is not a nice picture and, in fact, it lives up to the most frightening expectations etched in the minds of believers over the ages. Exactly how far into the future these events will take place is not known. But one thing is certain. Based on the words of Jesus and His servant Paul, we should know the times and seasons we are living in. And if that means anything it is that there will be signs to look for. Those signs are covered in book *#2: The Train of Warning Signs before the End Times.* That is why it is so important to gain a full appreciation that what we call the end times is, from its *beginning* moment, until the ending moment, *the day of the Lord.* With that understanding firmly planted it is then easy to find the details of events that will happen just before it begins. And it is necessary to understand those signs in order to understand the arrival of that season. This understanding also allows you to not be hyped by "teachers" selling products.

Knowing the Season

When Paul wrote to the Thessalonians he was clear about the need to watch so as not to be caught off guard by the launch of *the day of the Lord.* In 1 Thessalonians 5:1-6 he said:

> *¹But concerning the times and the seasons, brethren, you have no need that I should write to you. ² For you yourselves know perfectly that the day of the Lord so comes as a thief in the night. ³ For when they say, "Peace and safety!" then sudden destruction comes upon them, as labor pains upon a pregnant woman. And they shall not escape.*
>
> *⁴ But you, brethren, are not in darkness, so that this Day should overtake you as a thief. ⁵ You are all sons of light and sons*

> *of the day. We are not of the night nor of*
> *darkness.* **6** *Therefore let us not sleep, as*
> *others do, but let us watch and be sober.*

When he refers to *the times and the seasons* in this passage, he is referring to the time we popularly call the end times, although he does not use that phrase. However, he immediately associates those *times and seasons* with *the day of the Lord.* It is another way for him to say that the terribly difficult time, popularly referred to as the end times, is *the day of the Lord,* and this makes perfect sense based on what we have studied. Then Paul goes on to say that such *sudden destruction* should not catch the *sons of light* (God) unaware. In fact, he goes as far as to say that if the coming of the season of *the day of the Lord* does surprise them, then they are in a state of *darkness.* He is emphasizing that without a doubt we are to *watch and be sober so that that day does not overtake* (us) *as a thief.* And this clearly means that there will be signs unfolding just before it begins that will alert the children of light of its impending arrival. This admonition to recognize the season we are in is not to be confused with knowing *the day or the hour* of Christ's return which we cannot know.

Jesus adds His weight to this admonition in Revelation 3:3. While addressing the church at Sardis, of which He is unpleased, He tells them to watch lest, in addition to not knowing the hour, they will also be taken by surprise *as a thief.*

> *³ Remember therefore how you have received and heard; hold fast and repent. Therefore if you will not watch, I will come upon you as a thief, and you will not know what hour I will come upon you.*

There are several Scriptures in which we are told that no man knows *the day or the hour* that the Lord will return. But that truth is placed in the proper context with Jesus and Paul telling us to *watch* so that in addition to not knowing *the day or the hour,* we also won't be caught like *a thief* by not knowing *the times and the seasons.* In other words, they are making it clear we are to watch for signs so we are not surprised when the season arrives. That means there signs to see before its *beginning* and they are real and based on Scripture … not book selling hype. They are the signs that come just before the launch of *the day of the Lord* and are covered in detail in book *#2: The Train of Warning Signs before the End Times.*

With the foundation that the end times is *the day of the Lord* from start to finish established in this book, you will be prepared to read the next book which will describe, in detail, an array of VERY specific signs to look for that will unfold just before the end times begin. In addition to those specific signs there are also a number of general signs that must be in place for *the day of the Lord* (end times) to begin. But those general signs can go on for a period of time and are not as useful as the specific ones. Armed with this understand the believer will know the season when it comes and not be caught *like a thief in the night.*

CHAPTER SEVEN

What the *Beginning* of the End Times Looks Like

Chapter Hint: The events described in this chapter are a direct result of the conclusion that *the day of the Lord*, from start to finish, is what we popularly call the end times. It is also based on the establishment that *the day of the Lord* has a *beginning* phase called birth pangs. Based on those conclusions it is easy to describe the *beginning* of what is popularly called the end times.

Based on the various Scriptures we have looked at, relative to the *beginning* of *the day of the Lord* (end times), the following rendition is a representation of events that mark that horrific birth pangs phase. In more common language this is what the *beginning* of what we call the end times looks like. This description is only possible because of the conclusion that *the day of the Lord* is what we call the end times. All we need to do now is unpack the Scriptural descriptions of its birth pangs *beginning* phase.

Warfare

There is warfare, great warfare that starts suddenly and appears to be the dreaded World War III mankind has tried so hard to avoid. It is Jesus who leaves this impression by going out of His way to include the full spectrum government entities going to war with His, *nation shall rise against nation, and kingdom against kingdom* warning in Matthew 24:7-8. Within those Scriptures Jesus alerts us to the peaceful condition of the nations of the earth prior to this great-war by telling us they must *rise* when it begins. However, Paul is more specific in 1 Thessalonians 5:1-3 indicating its *beginning* will be *sudden*. Paul goes as far as to tell us the nations will embrace a delusion just before the great-war begins. They believe they have found *Peace*. However, this *Peace* will not flutter on the wings of angels, but only in the delusions of men. (Book #2 covers that *Peace* in detail.)

The apostle John, writing the Book of Revelation on the Isle of Patmos, describes this war as the *red horse*, loosed by the *second seal* which was loosened by the hand of Jesus from heaven. And the result of those nations and kingdoms suddenly rising to war is described broadly by John as taking *peace from the earth*. That is the *earth*, and not a part of it. Of course, what else should be expected from a horse of the apocalypse? Jeremiah 30, which also covers the birth pangs *beginning* of *the day of the Lord*, describes the degree to which *all nations* are dealt a severe blow by saying their fate is a *full end*. Although the nations of the earth are still around, they are devastated during this *beginning* phase. This depiction of that war brings to mind the words of Albert Einstein who said: "I know not with what weapons World War III will be fought, but World War IV will be fought with sticks and stones."

More Sorrows

Then in rapid succession John tells of the *black horse* and *pale horse* being loosened bringing *pestilence* and *famine* to a world wracked by warfare more deadly than any before it and confirming Jesus' admonitions in Matthew 24:7 of *famine* and *pestilence* in the *beginning of sorrows.* And there are *great* (the Greek word "megas") *earthquakes* occurring in *divers places* (all over) the earth according to Luke's rendition of the Olivet Discourse (Luke 21). This is in contrast to John the Revelator (Revelation 6) focusing on a particularly *great earthquake* that shakes the world. And why are there so many *great earthquakes* suddenly *beginning* all over the earth? Perhaps it is because we read in 2 Peter in the language of a first century man descriptions of what can only be detonations of nuclear weapons. Are those detonations triggering major fault lines of the earth? Luke adds the detail of the *sea and waves roaring.* Would this condition be the result of great earthquakes erupting on the sea floor as nations send nukes into the oceans to destroy nuclear submarines?

It is an incredibly destructive time with not even the heavens escaping the *wrath of the Lamb.* And surely this is His *wrath* since it is by the hand of Jesus in heaven that loosened the six seals launching the terrifying four horsemen. The KJV tells us the Lamb's *wrath is come* which is fairly obvious. But because it says "*is come,*" instead of "*has come*" as in the NKJV, some claim the four horsemen of the apocalypse were not His *wrath* even though they were unleashed by Jesus against the earth. They say this because they believe the Lord's wrath is yet to come since the verse reads *is come* in the KJV. They say this to fit their prophecy theories. However, they do not take such an approach when they say *He is risen* concerning Jesus' *resurrection*. And we all know that when we are told *He is risen*, it means He has *risen* and not that He is about to rise.

The Heavenly Condition

John in Revelation 6 is specific about the impact on the heavens at this time saying *the sun became black as sackcloth of hair, and the moon became as blood; And the stars of heaven fell unto the earth.* But it is Zephaniah who clears any question as to why all three, the *sun, moon,* and *stars,* are impacted <u>during</u> *the day of the Lord.* In Zephaniah 1:15 we are assured that *the day of the Lord is a day of wrath, a day of trouble and distress, a day of wasteness and desolation, <u>a day of darkness and gloominess, a day of clouds and thick darkness</u>.* And this is reiterated by the prophet Joel saying *the day of the Lord* is *a <u>day of darkness and of gloominess, a day of clouds and of thick darkness</u>.* And it is 2 Peter 3:10 where we likely discover why *the day of the Lord* is *a day of darkness and of gloominess, a day of clouds and thick darkness.*

> *But the day of the Lord will come as*
> *a thief in the night; in the which the*
> *heavens shall pass away with a great*
> *noise, and the elements shall melt with*
> *fervent heat, the earth also and the works*
> *that are therein shall be burned up.*

Similar to 1 Thessalonians 5:1-3 we see 2 Peter also use the phrase *a thief in the night* to indicate it is describing events in the *beginning* of *the day of the Lord.* That is because it is the prophetic birth pangs time frame of *the day of the Lord* that, we are told, *comes as a thief in the night.* And included within this description of this horrific *beginning* to *the day of the Lord* appears to be that of nuclear detonations, *the heavens shall pass away with a great noise, and the elements shall melt with fervent heat.* Apparently, there are enough nukes going off in the great-war that the atmosphere Zephaniah sees <u>during</u> *the day of the Lord* is one of *a day of clouds and thick darkness.* This would likely be the result of massive dust and smoke kicked up from multiple explosions. And this chain reaction of possible nukes would appear to be the cause of the great *clouds* and *thick darkness* which impacts the visibility of the *sun, moon, and stars* from the sight of earth dwellers. In Isaiah 13:10, which also has its focus on the *beginning* phase of *the day of the Lord,* even using a birth pangs term to establish it, the prophet describes the heavenly impact noting *the stars of heaven and the constellations thereof shall not give their light: the sun shall be darkened in his going forth, and the moon shall not cause her light to shine.*

Yet, there is great confusion within prophecy circles on this point. Most mix together the heavenly warning sign coming <u>before</u> the launch of *the day of the Lord,* (Joel 2:31) with the heavenly condition <u>during</u> *the day of the Lord* which we just observed. And this confusion ends any possibility of understanding the *beginning* of *the day of the Lord.* (End times) But there is something else transpiring during all of this tumult and it has to do with the Antichrist.

And as though all of these terrible trials were not enough we are told that as men gaze skyward they see *fearful sights and great signs* in the heavens. And along with these *fearful sights* shall be objects raining down upon the earth to the extent that man shall seek cover from *the stars of heaven* [falling] *unto the earth, even as a fig tree casteth her untimely figs, when she is shaken of a mighty wind.* And part of the *fearful sights* will be *the heaven*(s) [departing] *as a scroll when it is rolled together.* These descriptions make it likely that Scripture is describing a VERY

David Brennan

large asteroid or a VERY large comet passing VERY close to the earth. But we do not know for certain this is the case. However, the Biblical descriptions make such celestial objects the most likely to fulfill the Scriptural admonitions.

The Rise of Antichrist

If you are wondering when the Antichrist establishes his grip on the world look no further than this tumultuous time of prophetic birth pangs … the *beginning* phase of *the day of the Lord*. It is in Revelation 6 John sees *a white horse: and he that sat on him had a bow; and a crown was given unto him: and he went forth conquering, and to conquer.* This rider of the *white horse* in Revelation 6 is starkly different from Jesus riding a *white horse* in Revelation chapter 19, making it clear that the *white horse* unleashed in the *first seal* cannot be ridden by Christ. And this observation leaves the Antichrist as the only other realistic possibility.

The description of how the Antichrist rises to a place of world dominance is observed in the *first seal* with him *going forth conquering, and to conquer.* Some believe this *beast* empire is located in Europe and others in the Middle East.

He rides the *white horse* toward world domination leaving havoc and great destruction in his wake. And since we have identified the events described in Revelation 6 as taking place within the birth pangs (*beginning* phase) of *the day of the Lord,* that is when this *conquering* drive for world domination takes place. But how does he conquer the world? It appears to be from a uniquely deceptive method and with a lot of help according to Isaiah 13.

Isaiah 13 and the Conquerors

As we looked at previously Isaiah 13 begins with a reference to Babylon and then a few verses later reverts to *the day of the Lord.* The references to the heavenly condition being described in Isaiah 13 confirm the prophet is referring to the time of *the day of the Lord.* Isaiah also directly states in verse 5 *the day of the LORD is at hand; it shall come as a destruction from the Almighty.* Then two verses later he identifies where within the overall *day of the Lord* the events being described take place by using the clear birth pangs reference *they shall be in pain as a woman that travaileth.* And in that *beginning* phase of *the day of the Lord,* we know light from all (sun, moon, stars) heavenly bodies is impacted and this is reiterated in verse 10 describing *the stars of heaven and the constellations thereof shall not give their light: the sun shall be darkened in his going forth, and the moon shall not cause her light to shine.*

But Isaiah adds a detail not found in other Scriptures that focus on the *beginning* phase (birth pangs) of *the day of the Lord.* And this detail is very telling as to how the Antichrist appears to take down very powerful nations that would otherwise be impossible to defeat. Remember *the day of the Lord* is the time of God's wrath. And Isaiah actually tells us who the Lord will use as *the weapons of his indignation, to destroy the whole land* to launch the *beginning* of *the day of the Lord.*

> [5] *They come from a far country, from the end of heaven, even the* Lord, *and the weapons of his indignation, to destroy the whole land.*

Those used by the Lord to destroy the *whole land come from a far country.* That is correct. They come from a country that is far from the country they are living in at the time they *destroy the whole land.* They are foreigners.

Next we are told those the Lord uses from a *far country* will become like *the hunted gazelle, and as a sheep that no man takes up.* In other words, they are *hunted* and without any protection like the vulnerable *sheep.* And they respond as any people would. *And everyone will flee to his own land.*

> *14 It shall be as the hunted gazelle, And as a sheep that no man takes up; <u>Every man will turn to his own people, And everyone will flee to his own land.</u> 15 Everyone who is found will be thrust through, And everyone who is captured will fall by the sword. 16 Their children also will be dashed to pieces before their eyes; Their houses will be plundered And their wives ravished.*

And they *flee* for good reason. Because it was they whom were used by the Lord as *the weapons of his indignation, to destroy the whole land* and apparently the people in their host countries figured this out after the destruction takes place. So when these foreigners, who have brought so much destruction against their host countries are identified as the source of this destruction, this is what happens to them:

> *15 Everyone who is found will be thrust
> through, And everyone who is captured
> will fall by the sword. 16 Their children
> also will be dashed to pieces before their
> eyes; Their houses will be plundered And
> their wives ravished.*

Essentially, what Isaiah informs us is that the Antichrist will consume his enemies from within by using immigrants sympathetic to him/his cause to launch the attack. And there must be many of them plotting to do this harm against those who took them into their countries. But, in reality, it is the Lord using these foreigners to enact His wrath. Because we are told it is foreigners living within countries who are used by God against *all nations*, it is reasonable to see that the most vulnerable to this tactic are the Western democracies whose borders have been almost non-existent for several decades. And there is Scripture which appears to confirm the perspective that Western nations are hit the hardest out of *all nations*.

Western Nations

Adding to the case that during *the day of the Lord* Western nations are the ones struck hardest is Scripture found in the Book of Zephaniah. In chapter 1 starting in verse 15 some specific details concerning *the day of the Lord* are given. As we know of *that day* it will be a day of *wrath, trouble, distress, wasteness, desolation, darkness, gloominess and thick darkness.* Now consider these additional details provided in verses 16 and 18.

> *[16] A day of the trumpet and alarm against the <u>fenced cities</u>, and against the <u>high towers</u>. Zephaniah 1:16*

Verse 16 appears to be literally telling us that nations under the belief they are secure will be struck a terrible blow. They are nations that have *fenced cities,* which indicate notable protection. They also possess *high towers* along with those fences. Such towers are designed to provide a military intelligence advantage by allowing enemies to be seen from a distance. In other words, it appears that the nations being described here are the most prepared in terms of national defense. Now consider verse 18.

David Brennan

> [18]*Neither their silver nor gold shall be able to deliver them in the day of the Lord's wrath... Zephaniah 1:18*

Zephaniah also informs us that these nations possessing strong military defenses also possess great wealth and find that neither their strong military nor great wealth does them any good during *the day of the Lord.* To impart this understanding, he employs terms universally understood as indicating great wealth ... *silver* and *gold.* But the real significance of what is being relayed here is his identification of wealthy and well defended nations as the ones being struck. They are the ones that have the *silver* and *gold* and powerful militaries yet discover that during *the day of the Lord* it cannot deliver them from that great day of *wrath.* Why? Because the strike against them comes from within.

By Zephaniah identifying nations that have both great wealth as well as strong national defenses, we can now understand this to indicate what is referred to today as the Western powers.

It should be understood that nowhere within Zephaniah 1 is there any mention of birth pangs but, simply, as that of *the day of the Lord.*

86

CHAPTER EIGHT

Have Prophetic Birth Pangs Begun?

Chapter Hint: In this chapter it established that the world has not experience prophetic birth pangs yet. This is done by comparing the birth pang wars and earthquakes called for in Scripture, to the actual facts pertaining to both. This is necessary because individuals and ministries selling products to the church are claiming they have begun.

Some claim that prophetic birth pangs have already begun. But this mistake is a product of not understanding what birth pangs are. Based on Scripture we know they are the actual *beginning* of *the day of the Lord,* (end times) and we also know what happens when they begin. We know this according to Matthew 24:7, 1 Thessalonians 5:1-3,

Luke 21, and Revelation 6. We know that part of what happens is that there is a massive war between the nations of the earth which suddenly breaks out. We also know there are *great* (megas) *earthquakes in divers places* (all over) on the earth. So here are the facts concerning both of those signs.

Nation against Nation Warfare: Truth... not Hype

> "The period since 1945 arguably represents the longest period of <u>great power</u> peace since the birth of the modern world system in 1495."[1]

In a series of academic studies focusing on the phenomenon of war one thing is clear-warfare <u>between nations</u> has been trending down since the end of World War Two. In fact, one such study speculates that the current lack of warfare between nation-states might be at its lowest point since the year 1495! Those studies have led to articles with titles like, "Think Again: War...World Peace Could be Closer than you Think[2]" in the prestigious *Foreign Policy* magazine, and "War Really is Going Out of Style"[3] published in *The New York Times*.

However, this new condition among the nations does not mean warfare between nations has completely stopped, rather it is an indication the trend has been dramatically downward.

Warfare between the Nations

In searching for the true facts relating to nation-to-nation warfare consider the following quotes taken from a paper published in International Studies Quarterly (2003) titled: *Inter-State, Intra-State, and Extra-State Wars: A Comprehensive look at Their Distribution over Time, 1816-1997.* The study is a compilation of not less than 53 other studies on warfare that were produced by a multitude of academic scholars across the world. Read how clear they are about the subject of warfare between nations.

> [1]"the period since 1945 arguably represents the longest period of great power peace since the birth of the modern world system in 1495." Pp 52

> "world more peaceful than at any time in the past century." Pp 52

"Many scholars have noted a decreasing propensity for states to go to war. For instance, Levy detected a downward trend in great power wars (wars in which at least one major sovereign state fought on each of the two sides) over the period 1495–1975." Pp 51

"Discussions of the decline in warfare (between nations) have become more pronounced when dealing with the post–World War II era." Pp 51 If you are still not convinced then consider the following graph on battle deaths since the year 1946.[4]

Here are the references to those quotes:

[1] **Study Link:** http://deepblue.lib.umich.edu/bitstream/handle/2027.42/71639/1468-2478.4701003.pdf?sequence=1&isAllowed=y
[2] Foreignpolicy.com/2011/08/15/think-again-war/
[3] http://www.nytimes.com/2011/12/18/opinion/sunday/war-really-is-going-out-of-style.html?_r=0
[4] http://www.politifact.com/punditfact/statements/2014/jul/21/stu-burguiere/fewer-wars-fewer-people-dying-wars-now-quite-some/

Consider a chart reflecting the dramatic decline in "Battle Deaths" between the years 1946 and 2008 as a result of the dramatic decline in nation-to-nation warfare. The chart is from the Peace Research Institute of Oslo (PRIO)

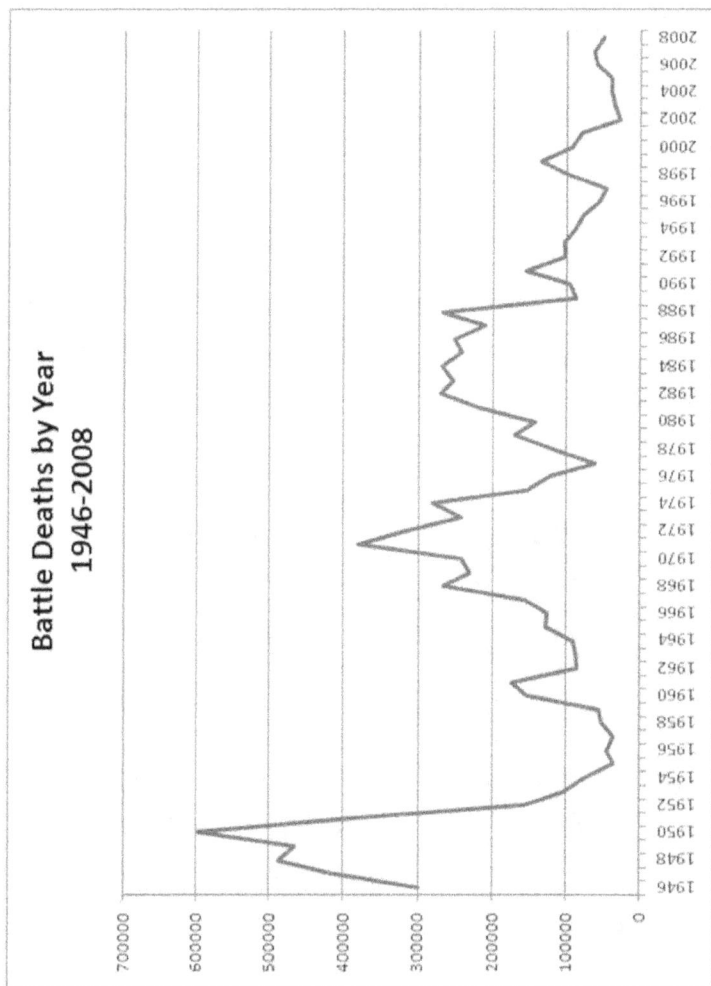

Now consider the true facts relating to earthquake activity across the world relative to if prophetic birth pangs have begun.

Are *Great Earthquakes in Divers Places* Occurring? Truth not hype.

Ask anyone who follows Bible prophecy if recent earthquake activity matches what the Scriptures tell us to look for and 9 out of 10 will offer an emphatic YES! But like so many traditions of men that circulate as truth, reality is quite different. First, consider again what the Scriptures have to say concerning the earthquakes that will accompany the start of the end times beginning with Matthew 24:6-8.

> *6 And ye shall hear of wars and rumours of wars: see that ye be not troubled: for all these things must come to pass, but the end is not yet.*
>
> *7 For nation shall rise against nation, and kingdom against kingdom: and there shall be famines, and pestilences, <u>and earthquakes, in divers places.</u>*

⁸ All these are the beginning of sorrows.

As we saw earlier Matthew tells us the signs that accompany the start of the end times in verse 7 and we are told *earthquakes* will be taking place *in divers places.* The word used for *divers* is the Greek preposition kata which means "though out." So we are told earthquakes will be occurring throughout the world when *the day of the Lord* (End times) launches. But since earthquakes have been taking place throughout the Earth for thousands of years this Scripture alone doesn't really help. All we know from it is that there will be earthquakes all over the earth. However, Luke 21:9-11, which covers the same end time *beginning* events as Matthew 24:6-8, adds a detail to the type of earthquakes that will be happening allowing us to become much more precise in what to look for.

> *⁹ But when ye shall hear of wars and commotions, be not terrified: for these things must first come to pass; but the end is not by and by.*

> ¹⁰ *Then said he unto them, Nation shall rise against nation, and kingdom against kingdom:*
>
> ¹¹ *<u>And great earthquakes shall be in divers places</u>, and famines, and pestilences; and fearful sights and great signs shall there be from heaven.*

Here we are provided a significant qualifier that eliminates the overwhelming majority of earthquakes that take place each year. We are told the earthquakes that will be all over the earth at the launch of the end times will be *great* ones. So to determine exactly what is meant by the term *great* let's look at how it is used elsewhere in Luke.

The term *great* is used 38 times in the Book of Luke to describe either something or someone that is extraordinary. For example, in Luke 1:15 John the Baptist is referred to as *great*. In Luke 1:32 Jesus is referred to as *great* as well as the multitudes that followed Jesus in Luke 5:15. The word used for *great* is the Greek adjective "megas" the same word that produces our English word "mega" for something that is incredibly large or significant. The key understanding here is that this term is used to impart an exceptional nature to that which it is being applied. So the earthquakes associated with the launch of *the day of the Lord* will be extraordinarily significant ones. They will be "mega" earthquakes. Now consider what the United States Geological Survey (U.S.G.S.) says about "mega" earthquakes over the last 100 years.

In an article published on April 17, 2016 after a series of earthquakes rocked Japan and Ecuador, the U.S.G.S. indicated there have been <u>no</u> "mega" earthquakes since seismic activity has been measured over the last 100 years. And this statement was issued after earthquakes of 7.3 and 7.8 had just been recorded.

Strong's Concordance

<u>Great:</u> Greek adjective "megas"

Dictionary.com

<u>English Word "Mega":</u> From the Greek word "megas" for huge, powerful, great

David Brennan

U.S.G.S. Statement on "Mega" Quakes

On the U.S.G.S. website the following is a good summation of their answer to the question if "mega" earthquakes are even possible:

> "Theoretically yes, but realistically the answer is probably no... Scientists, however, can't rule out a "mega" quake because they've only been measuring earthquakes for 100 years.

But for the sake of this article and for those who insist on their own definition of what constitutes *great* (megas) *earthquakes,* consider the following two graphs of 8.0 and higher earthquake activity by decade between the years 1900 and 2000 and then annual earthquake activity since 1995.

8.0+ Earthquakes Per Decade Since 1900

8.0+ Earthquakes Per Year Since 1995

To verify these results simply go the following link and you can plug-in the criteria yourself. http://earthquake.usgs.gov/earthquakes/search/

It is clear from those graphs that significant earthquakes have not been increasing across the earth since the year 1900. And something else to consider. In the first three or four decades of the last century, there were not many seismometers across the world. As a result some number of large earthquakes went unrecorded. So the numbers during that time are understated which further emphasizes the lack of increasing great earthquake activity. And remember, the Scriptural requirement for earthquake activity that accompanies the start of birth pangs is *great* (mega) *earthquakes* all over the surface of the earth. Since this is what the Scriptures call for, and the above graphs are an accurate reflection of the lack of mega or *great earthquakes* across the earth, it is easy to reach a solid non-hyped conclusion: No… as of the year 2018 the earthquakes required when birth pangs begin have not yet begun.

Famines

As we know from Jesus' words in the Olivet Discourse when prophetic birth pangs begin it will also include notable famine. Additionally, the famine mentioned by Jesus in the opening scene of the end times is also mentioned by John in Revelation as arriving by the rider of the *black horse*. So there is little doubt Scripture is talking about famine on a scale that the world has never before seen. Now consider the following chart reflecting the trend famine has taken across the globe since the year 1900. The chart is produced by the International Food Policy Research Institute.

As the chart clearly shows, not only is there no notable famine on the earth over the last 100 years, in fact, world famine has declined dramatically disproving any claims that the famines associated with the birth pangs of the end times have begun.

Since the signs of prophetic birth pangs come suddenly and with a great-war, and this great-war between nations and kingdoms reflects the red horse of Revelation, and none of the additional horrors that will be associated with that great-war are present, then the results of these statistics was to be expected. Clearly, the world will know without a doubt when the birth pangs of the end times begin.

Death toll from great famines in millions

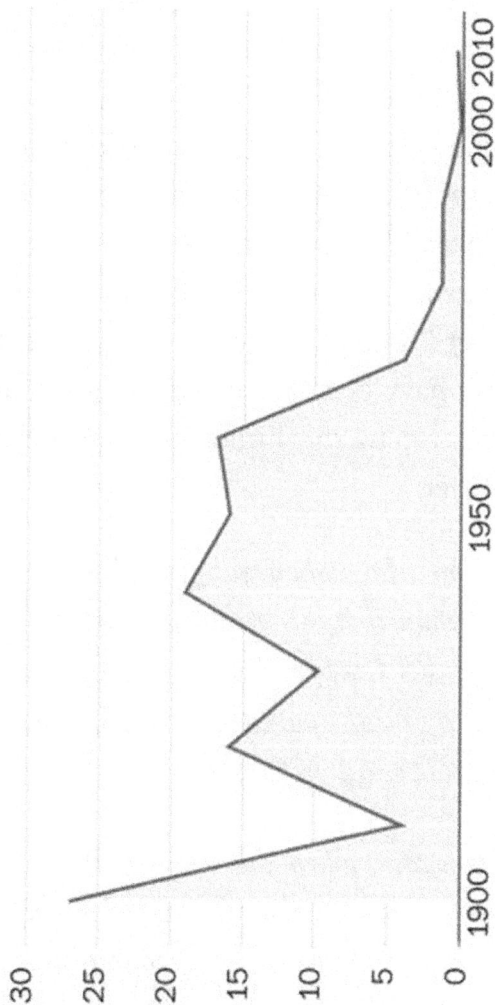

Note: Each great famine killed more than 100,000 people.

Sources: International Food Policy Research Institute,
U.S. Census Bureau (2013a, 2013b); World Peace Foundation (2015).   THE WASHINGTON POST

David Brennan

Sensationalism Alert

Some try to find events across a length of time that meet the qualifications of what we read in the Olivet Discourse and the Book of Revelation. One way they do this is to connect major historical events that span many decades or even centuries. It is an effort to make things fit by simply expanding the time frame covered. However, here is the Scriptural problem with that approach. In all three recordings of Jesus' Olivet Discourse, after all of its events from start to finish have been presented, we are told the following relative to the limitation of time those events will cover:

> *33 So you also, when you see all these things, know that it is near—at the doors! 34 Assuredly, I say to you, <u>this generation will by no means pass away till all these things take place</u>.* Matthew 24:33-34

> *31 So you also, when you see these things happening, know that the kingdom of God is near. 32 Assuredly, I say to you, <u>this generation will by no means pass away till all things take place</u>.* Luke 21:31-32

²⁹ So you also, when you see these things happening, know that it is near—at the doors! ³⁰ Assuredly, I say to you, <u>this generation will by no means pass away till all these things take place</u>. Mark 13:29-30

We are being told that the events covered in the Olivet Discourse, from the *beginning* moment of what we call the end times, until the last moment, that once they begin they will take place within a single generation. So don't be fooled by those taking the approach of expanding the time frame in order to make the events fit.

The Last Word

It is clear that the *beginning* of the end times is, in reality, the *beginning* of *the day of the Lord*. And for the sake of accuracy this is how it should be referred to. In reaching this conclusion we receive a clear indication of major events that will take place when it begins. And the consistency of descriptions of the *beginning* found in multiple Scriptures lends more credibility to the notion that we have isolated the *beginning* events. And this is important because with this foundation we can avoid basic errors that appear to plague many Bible prophecy concepts.

One of the benefits of identifying that *the day of the Lord* is, in reality, what we call the end times, is that we are then able to identify several major signs that will take place before it begins. And the details of some of these signs differ from what is believed by some students of Bible prophecy. These signs are identified in *#2: The Train of Warning Signs before the End Times.* By understanding these signs the

105

Christian is equipped to discern between real and fake prophecy signs.

Considering how many fake prophecies there have been since the year 2000, this is a real benefit derived from understanding that *the day of the Lord* is, in reality, what we call the end times.

I hope this book has been a blessing to you and others. It is designed to form a secure Scriptural foundation for understanding the next four books in this series. Because once the student of Bible prophecy has this foundation, established by multiple Scriptures, taken literally, and in context, he or she can securely move forward in understanding.

God bless,
David Brennan

Addendum 1: Refuting those who say Revelation 6 cannot be *the day of the Lord* because of heavenly signs.

Although Revelation 6 fits well with what we see in Matthew 24:7-8 and also within 1 Thessalonians 5:1-3, some say it cannot be the *beginning* of *the day of the Lord* (God's wrath). They feel compelled to take this position because they see a heavenly sign near the end of the chapter that they believe is the same one found in the Book of Acts and the Book of Joel that comes <u>before</u> *the day of the Lord* begins. This is how those warnings read:

> Acts 2:20 & Joel 2:31
>
> The <u>sun shall be turned into darkness,</u> <u>And the moon into blood,</u> **Before** the *coming of the great and awesome day of* the LORD.

We are told that <u>before</u> *the day of the Lord* (God's wrath) begins a heavenly sign will appear. That sign is a darkening sun and a moon that turns to blood. Exactly what these are we cannot be certain. But it is contended by some that the events in Revelation 6 cannot be the start of *the day of the Lord* (God's wrath) because the heavenly sign coming <u>before</u> *the day of the Lord* is near the end of the chapter. Therefore, they say, *the day of the Lord* must start sometime after Revelation 6. Here is the verse in Revelation 6 used to support their conclusion.

Revelation 6:12-13

> ¹² *I looked when He opened the sixth seal, and behold, there was a great earthquake; and <u>the sun became black as sackcloth of hair, and the moon became like blood.</u>* ¹³ <u>*And the stars of heaven fell to the earth,*</u> *as a fig tree drops its late figs when it is shaken by a mighty wind.*

As can be seen in these verses there is a heavenly sign at the end of Revelation 6 similar to the warning signs noted in Acts and Joel. And at first glance this appears to be the same heavenly sign that comes **before** *the day of the Lord* begins. But there is a problem with that perspective. The heavenly sign mentioned in Acts and Joel includes only the sun and moon but not the stars. However, in Revelation 6:12-13, the sun, moon, and stars are mentioned. Also we are <u>not</u> told this sign in Revelation 6 is <u>*before* the day</u> *of the Lord* begins which both Joel and Acts tell us. And the reason for these differences is this.

The heavenly signs coming *before the day of the Lord* in Acts and Joel is, indeed, a warning coming just *before* God's wrath begins. But the one near the end of Revelation 6 refers to a heavenly <u>condition</u> that develops <u>during</u> *the day of the Lord*. It is an atmospheric condition that causes the sun, moon and stars to be impacted. The following verses support that <u>during</u> *the day of the Lord* the atmosphere is impacted.

Zephaniah 1:15

¹⁵That day is a day of wrath, A day of trouble and distress,

A day of devastation and desolation, <u>day</u> <u>of darkness and gloominess,</u>

<u>A day of clouds and thick darkness,</u>

Joel 2: 2

**<u>² A day of darkness and gloominess, A day
of clouds and thick darkness,</u>**

Because *the day of the Lord* is *a day of clouds
and thick darkness,* naturally all celestial bodies are
impacted. And wherever in Scripture you see the *sun,
moon,* and *stars* impacted in association with *the day
of the Lord* this is the reason why. This distinction
between the heaven sign coming before *the day of the
Lord* begins, and the heavenly condition during *the
day of the Lord,* is the reason some people think *the
day of the Lord* begins only after Revelation 6.

Addendum 2: Scriptures proving that the correct definition of the day of the Lord is "the time of God's wrath on the earth."

Amos 5:18-20

Alas, you who are longing for the day of the LORD, For what purpose will the day of the LORD be to you? It will be darkness and not light; As when a man flees from a lion And a bear meets him, Or goes home, leans his hand against the wall And a snake bites him. Will not the day of the LORD be darkness instead of light, Even gloom with no brightness in it?

Ezekiel 30:3-4

"For the day is near, Even the day of the LORD is near; It will be a day of clouds, A time of doom for the nations. "A sword will come upon Egypt, And anguish will be in Ethiopia; When the slain fall in Egypt, They take away her wealth, And her foundations are torn down.

Isaiah 2:12

For the LORD of hosts will have a day of reckoning Against everyone who is proud and lofty And against everyone who is lifted up, That he may be abased.

Isaiah 13:9-10

Behold, the day of the LORD is coming, Cruel, with fury and burning anger, To make the land a desolation; And He will exterminate its sinners from it. For the stars of heaven and their constellations Will not flash forth their light; The sun will be dark when it rises And the moon will not shed its light.

Isaiah 24:21-22

So it will happen in that day, That the LORD will punish the host of heaven on high, And the kings of the earth on earth. They will be gathered together Like prisoners in the dungeon, And will be confined in prison; And after many days they will be punished.

Joel 3:12-14

Let the nations be aroused And come up to the valley of Jehoshaphat, For there I will sit to judge All the surrounding nations. Put in the sickle, for the harvest is ripe Come, tread, for the wine press is full; The vats overflow, for their wickedness is great. Multitudes, multitudes in the valley of decision! For the day of the LORD is near in the valley of decision.

Joel 1:15

Alas for the day! For the day of the LORD is near, And it will come as destruction from the Almighty.

Joel 2:2-4

A day of darkness and gloom, A day of clouds and thick darkness As the dawn is spread over the mountains, So there is a great and mighty people; There has never been anything like it, Nor will there be again after it To the years of many generations. A fire consumes before them And behind them a flame burns The land is like the garden of Eden before them But a desolate wilderness behind them, And nothing at all escapes them. Their appearance is like the appearance of horses; And like war horses, so they run.

Jeremiah 30:7-8

'Alas! for that day is great, There is none like it; And it is the time of Jacob's distress, But he will be saved from it. 'It shall come about on that day,' declares the LORD of hosts, 'that I will break his yoke from off their neck and will tear off their bonds; and strangers will no longer make them their slaves.

Malachi 4:1

"For behold, the day is coming, burning like a furnace; and all the arrogant and every evildoer will be chaff; and the day that is coming will set them ablaze," says the LORD of hosts, "so that it will leave them neither root nor branch."

Obadiah 1:15-16

"For the day of the LORD draws near on all the nations As you have done, it will be done to you Your dealings will return on your own head. "Because just as you drank on My holy mountain, All the nations will drink continually. They will drink and swallow And become as if they had never existed.

2 Peter 3:10

But the day of the Lord will come like a thief, in which the heavens will pass away with a roar and the elements will be destroyed with intense heat, and the earth and its works will be burned up.

2 Peter 3:11-12

Since all these things are to be destroyed in this way, what sort of people ought you to be in holy conduct and godliness, looking for and hastening the coming of the day of God, because of which the heavens will be destroyed by burning, and the elements will melt with intense heat!

Revelation 6:15-17

Then the kings of the earth and the great men and the commanders and the rich and the strong and every slave and free man hid themselves in the caves and among the rocks of the mountains; and they said to the mountains and to the rocks, "Fall on us and hide us from the presence of Him who sits on the throne, and from the wrath of the Lamb; for the great day of their wrath has come, and who is able to stand?"

1 Thessalonians 5:2-3

For you yourselves know full well that the day of the Lord will come just like a thief in the night. While they are saying, "Peace and safety!" then destruction will come upon them suddenly like labor pains upon a woman with child, and they will not escape.

Zephaniah 1:14-18

Near is the great day of the LORD, Near and coming very quickly; Listen, the day of the LORD! In it the warrior cries out bitterly. A day of wrath is that day, A day of trouble and distress, A day of destruction and desolation, A day of darkness and gloom, A day of clouds and thick darkness, A day of trumpet and battle cry Against the fortified cities And the high corner towers.

Zephaniah 3:8

"Therefore wait for Me," declares the LORD, "For the day when I rise up as a witness Indeed, My decision is to gather nations, To assemble kingdoms, To pour out on them My indignation, All My burning anger; For all the earth will be devoured By the fire of My zeal.

Zechariah 14:2

For I will gather all the nations against Jerusalem to battle, and the city will be captured, the houses plundered, the women ravished and half of the city exiled, but the rest of the people will not be cut off from the city.

Zephaniah 1:18

Neither their silver nor their gold Will be able to deliver them On the day of the LORD'S wrath; And all the earth will be devoured In the fire of His jealousy, For He will make a complete end, Indeed a terrifying one, Of all the inhabitants of the earth.

Zephaniah 2:3

Seek the LORD, All you humble of the earth Who have carried out His ordinances; Seek righteousness, seek humility <u>Perhaps you will be hidden In the day of the LORD'S anger.</u>